Introduction

In 1839, three men from England exited a boat ⟨...⟩ a little town called East Liverpool, Ohio. They were ⟨...⟩.

The curiosity of the residents of East Liverpoo⟨...⟩ e next morning, bought a pick and shovel and started for the hills. On the hillside of what is now known as Jethro Hill, they dug out some dirt, which they dried and ground in an old coffee mill. They then mixed a batch and in a small kiln they constructed, fired a test batch. The results of the test must have satisfied them, for they bought some land along the river bank and shortly thereafter started East Liverpool's first pottery.

Their first ventures were Rockingham and Yellowware. They continued with this product very successfully until about 1844, when they sold the business to the Croxall Brothers. The Croxall Brothers operated the business until about 1852, when a large flood struck the area and washed away sections of the river banks and part of the plant.

In 1853, Isaac Knowles and Isaac Harvey operated a "store boat", selling pottery and glass and staples along the Ohio and Mississippi rivers. In 1854, Isaac Knowles and Isaac Harvey purchased what remained of the buildings and used the old lumber to build a kiln. They also produced Rockingham and Yellowware. Isaac Knowles first invention was a Rockingham type fruit jar with a tin lid, an idea he patented, which sold with a pie plate of the same material. Isaac built up quite a trade with his invention, which he produced and sold for many years.

Around 1870 Isaac Harvey left the business and a partnership was formed which was the beginning of one of the most innovative pottery companies in the United States at that time. The partnership consisted of Isaac Knowles, his son Homer, and Colonel John N. Taylor, who was married to the daughter of Isaac Knowles.

They discontinued production of the Rockingham wares and after many trials and errors drew their first kiln of whiteware on September 5, 1872. It was considered quite a successful venture and, by 1900, theirs was the largest pottery in the United States, employing over 700 people.

WORKS OF KNOWLES, TAYLOR & KNOWLES, EAST LIVERPOOL

Chapter 1
Knowles, Taylor & Knowles Belleek
Circa 1889

BELLEEK

In 1886, the *Crockery and Glass Journal* announced that the firm of Knowles, Taylor & Knowles was experimenting with the production of a fine china. The word was out that the firm was attempting to produce china ware that would rival the best.

In the early history of the American potteries, no fine china had been produced in the United States. Any china purchased in the United States had a foreign stamp and was considered inferior if not marked French or English. It was the dream of the management of Knowles, Taylor & Knowles to produce a china that would be the pride of America.

An extensive search for an individual who had the knowledge needed to assist in the production of this fine china was underway. The services of Joshua Poole, an authority on the production of bone china and the previous manager of the Belleek Pottery Limited in County Fermanagh, Ireland, were employed.

Joshua Poole worked under complete secrecy; his experiments were successful and a high quality bone china became a reality for Knowles, Taylor & Knowles.

Bone china is made by adding bone ash as an ingredient to the porcelain composition. Bone ash consists of burned animal bones crushed into a fine powder which is pure white in color. English porcelain makers discovered this combination of ingredients about 1750. Hard porcelain, though strong, chips fairly easily and unless specially treated is usually tinged with blue or gray. Whereas bone china is strong, it does not chip easily and has an ivory-white appearance. The bone ash greatly increases the translucence and whiteness of the porcelain. Bone china is also less expensive to make.

In early 1888 an announcement was made in the *Crockery and Glass Journal* that the firm of Knowles, Taylor & Knowles was building a plant that was to produce a fine china. The plant was erected at Walnut and Bradshaw Avenue in East Liverpool, Ohio.

On February 11, 1889, the East Liverpool *Daily Crisis* ran an article that stated "The firm of Knowles, Taylor & Knowles has trouble at the new works that has not yet been rectified and little is being done. It is said that the first kiln of the new china ware that was fired, proved a total loss, being of such quality that it was not fit to be shipped. It is to be hoped that the trouble will soon be over so that the large establishment can start up in full blast." It seems that the entry into fine china production was not proving to be an easy task.

In May 1889 the *Crockery and Glass Journal* stated that "The firm of Knowles, Taylor & Knowles was introducing an item called K.T.K. BELLEEK, a delicate and translucent china". The announcement must have been an emotional time for the management of the Knowles, Taylor & Knowles firm and for Joshua Poole, whose experiments were now becoming a reality.

Knowles, Taylor & Knowles

16 95

American Bone China

With Price Guide

Timothy J. Kearns

77 Lower Valley Road, Atglen, PA 19310

edication

To my loving wife, Cheryl, without whom
this book would have only been a dream

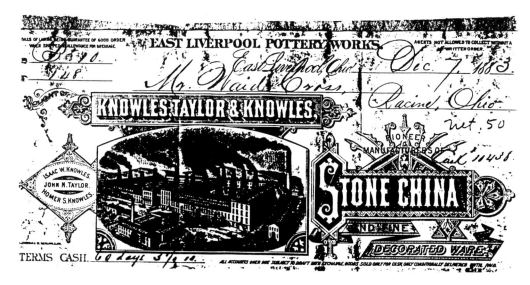

Printed in the United States of America
ISBN: 0-88740-636-X

We are interested in hearing from authors
with book ideas on related topics.

Published by Schiffer Publishing Ltd.
77 Lower Valley Road
Atglen, PA 19310
Please write for a free catalog.
This book may be purchased from the
publisher.
Please include $2.95 postage.
Try your bookstore first.

Contents

Acknowledgements

As with all books that have been written throughout the years, no one author can do it all. It begins with a thought, then the desire to do the task, and numerous other people to make the book successful. To those who assisted in the making of this book, I owe a sincere debt of gratitude.

Charles and Dorothy Bechtol, Ohio
Paul H. Blair, Ohio
Perry Crandall, Ohio
East Liverpool Museum of Ceramics, East Liverpool, Ohio
Barbara Edmonson, Chico, California, Author of "Old Advertising Spirits Glasses"
Courtney Frioux, Louisiana
William C. Gates Jr., Ohio Historical Society, Columbus, Ohio
Larry Gleba, Photographer, Lyndhurst, Ohio
Cheryl Kearns, Ohio
Martha Lyden, Ohio
Mary Och, Ohio
Ohio Historical Society, Columbus, Ohio
Philip Rickerd, Ceramic Museum of East Liverpool, Ohio
Robert Snyder, Snyder Whiskey Research Center, Amarillo, Tx
Jack Sullivan, Alexandria, Virginia
William E. White, Ohio
Wolf's Fine Arts Auctioneers, Cleveland, Ohio
Carol Wykoff, Ohio

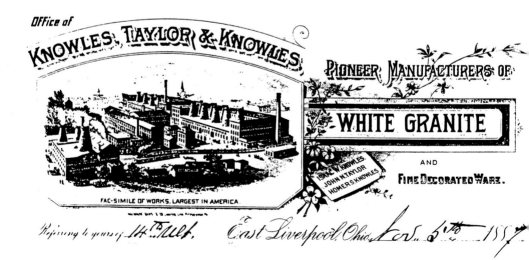

Original Belleek catalog page from an 1889
Knowles, Taylor & Knowles display. A special
thank you to the Ceramic Museum of East
Liverpool, Ohio for allowing us to photograph this
original page of the Belleek catalog.

Unfortunately, on November 11, 1889, a natural gas explosion caused the new china works plant of Knowles, Taylor & Knowles to be totally destroyed. All the stock of Belleek and the molds were lost in the devastation of the fire.

Knowles, Taylor & Knowles Belleek china had a short history. Today, to find a piece marked K.T.K. Belleek is rare. Very few pieces survived the short production period and the destruction from the fire.

7

Chapter 2
Lotus Ware
Circa 1892-1896

In the spring of 1890 the new china producing plant was finished and ready for production. Under the capable hands of Joshua Poole, who had been manager of the Belleek Pottery Limited in Ireland - famous for its fine china, the firm of Knowles, Taylor & Knowles was again producing fine china.

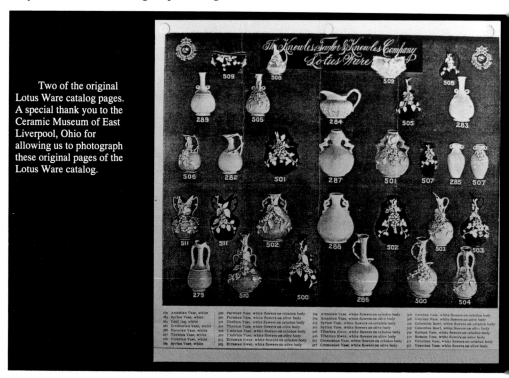

Two of the original Lotus Ware catalog pages. A special thank you to the Ceramic Museum of East Liverpool, Ohio for allowing us to photograph these original pages of the Lotus Ware catalog.

On June 2, 1892, the *Crockery and Glass Journal* ran an article stating that the firm of Knowles, Taylor & Knowles was again producing fine art china.

On June 23, 1892 the same trade paper ran an article stating that the firm of Knowles, Taylor & Knowles now had three marks that they were using: Iron Stone China mark; K.T.K./China mark; and K.T.K. Lotus Ware mark.

On June 30, 1892 the *Crockery and Glass Journal* stated the firm of Knowles, Taylor & Knowles had introduced their fine china ware under the name "Lotus Ware". This is the first known reference to the name "Lotus Ware". Until this announcement, the fine china items were thought to be marked K.T.K./CHINA.

In 1893, the beautiful new art china of the Knowles, Taylor & Knowles Co. was introduced at the World's Columbia Exposition in Chicago by Colonel John N. Taylor. It was a proud day for a small pottery company from East Liverpool, Ohio, that was predominant at the time only in the manufacture of vitreous hotel china.

Lotus Ware has two known marks, both colored green. One is a circle with a crown on top and Lotus Ware printed around the outside. Inside are the initials K.T.K. Co., with a crescent and a star. The second known mark is similar with the words Knowles, Taylor & Knowles spelled out.

The bodies of Lotus Ware are light, translucent and fragile. The body colors are a gloss or matte finished white and the rare, light or dark green. Lotus Ware expresses the Art Nouveau influence of the era, with its flowing body styles and applied decorations.

The vases and bowls and other items made in the casting shop were then taken to the kilns to be fired for the first time. After the firing took place, the items were sent to the decorating shop to be decorated partially or totally by hand. There the skilled artists gilded the ware or applied hand painted designs. Once decorated, the item was fired again to render the design permanent. The wares were then sent to the warehouse.

An applied method of decoration unique to Lotus Ware was used for placing flowers, leaves, stems and filigree (open works of elaborate designs) on the body of the china. This method has been attributed to Mr. Henry Schmidt, a German artist hired by the firm of Knowles, Taylor & Knowles.

Will T. Blake, assistant to Mr. Schmidt, stated in a letter,

"Mr. Schmidt originated his own floral decorations and open work designs. When he was ready to put his clay flowers on a Lotus bowl, he would first center the bowl on a whirler and then trace out his particular pattern on the bowl with an undulating movement, much like one would trace an imaginary lead pencil around the bowl. His instruments were a rubber bag and copper tube similar to that used in cake decorating. The stems, leaves, and flowers of his patterns were produced with remarkable skill. He used a small piece of plaster of Paris, a little bit thicker than a lead pencil and shaped like a petal, to give a more realistic impression to his flowers. This was always done after the clay petals had reached the proper hardness. The stems of these floral designs, and sometimes the leaves that were attached to them, were indented with a sharp tool to give a roughened and more natural effect to them.

His open work patterns were first worked out on a small plaster mold. He would do a quick penciling of his design on the mold and then etch it out slowly with his cornucopia bag, these minute indentations served to support the moist clay while the clay was drying. When the drying process was complete, the open work would be removed from the mold by a slight jolt on the plaster form from the hand.

He would next take the open work designs into his hand and apply a little fresh slip to its outer edges. Then he would attach the design to the vase or bowl he was working on. If too much pressure were applied, the pattern would be crushed and rendered useless."

"Jewelling" was another decorative mechanism used often with the effect of a jewel and swag type chain on the Lotus Ware pieces.

"Fishnet" is seen on many Lotus Ware pieces as a netting type design molded into the piece. The fishnet design was used like other molded designs which imitated forms such as shells and leaves.

Many pieces were decorated at the factory and others were decorated outside the factory by amateurs and professionals alike. It was fashionable at the time to purchase items through retail or wholesale outlets and paint them as a hobby or as a business. Even for long time collectors, it is a difficult task to know whether a piece was factory decorated. Some of the factory artists are known through pictures of old employees or from people who remembered them and have passed down the information. Many artists were rovers and did not stay long at any one place.

The dates on artist marked pieces cause much confusion, especially when the date is from the period of Lotus Ware production. It is thought that most factory artists did not mark their pieces because they were paid for each completed piece and it would be too costly to take the time to initial and date each piece. It was easy for the amateur artist to paint a piece, initial it, and have a friend at one of the many factories in East Liverpool fire it for them.

After the reign of Lotus Ware, the excess stock was sold to artists through the factory or outlets. This is the reason for many of the various dates on marked pieces included here. An ad placed in the East Liverpool Review in December of 1908 states "On sale Saturday, We (Newmon's Bazaar) have purchased from the firm of Knowles, Taylor & Knowles, one thousand seven hundred eighty pieces of the famous Lotus Ware to be sold to individuals at excellent prices".

The period of production of some of the finest bone china ever manufactured in America was brief. The high expense of production and the costly losses in the firing of the wares brought the manufacture of Lotus Ware, the dream of the management of the firm of Knowles, Taylor & Knowles, to a halt in late 1895 or early 1896. The exact date is not known.

Today collectors who own a piece of Lotus Ware may be assured that they have one of the finest pieces of art china that this country has ever produced.

Lotus Ware Shell Tray - Large shell with ruffled edges and tri-footed base - Artist signed: M.A.B. Width 8 1/2"

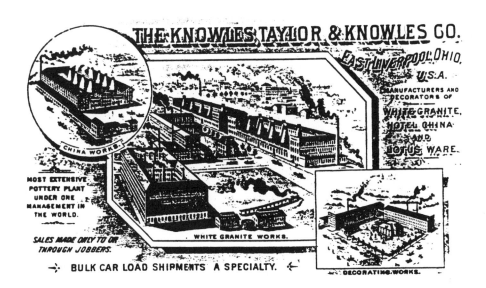

Lotus Ware Etruscan Vase - Bulbous body with
slender neck and applied scrolled handles - Height
8"

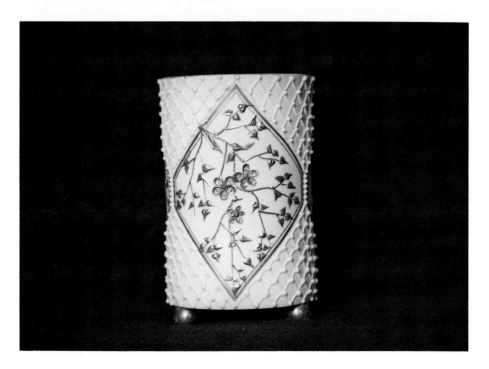

Lotus Ware Tuscan Vase - Cylindrical style with
fishnet pattern on tri-footed base - Height 8"

Lotus Ware Perfume Ewer - Round ewer with
ruffled rim and footed base - Handle missing -
Height 3 1/2"

Lotus Ware Valenciennes Jug - Fishnet pattern
with twig handle - Height 3 3/4"

Lotus Ware Fern Jardiniere - Deep rounded bowl
with ruffled mouth and applied twig handle - Hand
painted flower design with garlands of roses inside
- Artist signed: R.B. - Height 5 1/2"

Lotus Ware Etruscan Ewer - Bulbous body with slender neck, scroll handle and spout lip - Applied white flowers, leaves and stems - Height 9 1/2"

Lotus Ware Perfume Ewer - Round ewer with ruffled rim and footed base - Handle missing - Height 3 1/2"

Lotus Ware Deccan Jar - Bulbous body with raised
filigree medallions on sides with four petal type
feet - Lid has raised filigree with rosettes and finial
- Height 7 1/4"

Lotus Ware Thebian Vase - Double gourd shaped
form with applied step form handles - Height
8 1/4"

Lotus Ware Columbia Bowl - Bulbous body with fishnet pattern and ruffled rim - Artist signed: B.E. Weeks - Height 4 1/4"

Lotus Ware Cracker Jar - Beige jar with flowers and berry design - Lid is matching design - Height 6 1/2"

Lotus Ware Etruscan Ewer - Bulbous body with
slender neck and spout lip - Applied scroll handle -
Height 10"

Lotus Ware Bon Nappies - Large dish with leaf
pattern and ruffled rim - Four twig footed base -
Height 2"

Lotus Ware Valenciennes Jug - Fishnet pattern
with twig handle - Height 4 1/2"

Lotus Ware Cracker Jar - Fishnet pattern with
matching lid - Height 6 3/4"

Lotus Ware Venetian Vase - V-shaped form neck with applied handles - Old man of the mountain design on sides with petal design near lip and columned base - Artist signed: M.A.T. 1903 - Height 8"

Lotus Ware Columbia Bowl - Fishnet pattern with ruffled rim - Height 4"

Lotus Ware Venice Teapot, Sugar and Creamer set
- Raised pastel flowers with ribbed middle and
notched rims - Applied handles have unique inner
arched pieces attached to base - Height of Teapot
5 1/4"

Lotus Ware Lily Vase - Formed lily with applied
stems and leaves - Height 8 3/4"

Lotus Ware Cracker Jar - Raised painted berries
and flowers with branches and leaves - Lid is
matching - Height 6 3/4"

Lotus Ware Shell Tray - Medium shell with ruffled edges and tri-stemmed feet - Width 5"

Opposite Page Photo: Lotus Ware Etruscan Ewer - Bulbous body with long slender neck to pour spout and applied scrolled handle - Raised filigree ribbing around body with beaded ridge mid-ewer and beaded columns from middle to top - Height 9 3/4"

Lotus Ware Umbrian Vase - Bulbous body with short neck to flared top and applied scrolled handles - Artist signed: C.E.F. 1895 - Height 8 1/4"

Lotus Ware Leaf Jug - Leaf pattern with applied
twig handle - Height 5"

Lotus Ware Valenciennes Teapot, Sugar and
Creamer - Fishnet pattern with applied twig
handles and matching lids - Height of Teapot
5 1/4"

Lotus Ware Etruscan Vase - Bulbous body with long slender neck to flared top and applied scrolled handles - Two raised filigree medallions on body with raised beaded base and beaded columns from middle to top with rosettes - Resembles Carnival type glass with its mirror finish - Height 9"

Lotus Ware Tuscan Vase - Cylindrical style with fishnet pattern on tri-footed base - Height 8"

Lotus Ware Globe Jug - Flower and thorn branches throughout body with applied twig handle - Height 5"

Lotus Ware Columbia Bowl - Bulbous body with
beaded ruffled rim and beaded ring near top with
flower pattern - Applied filigree medallions on
sides - Height 4 1/2"

Lotus Ware Umbrian Vase - Bulbous body with
short neck to flared top and applied scrolled
handles - Height 8 1/4"

Lotus Ware Parmian Vase - Bulbous body with long slender neck to flared ridged top - Swirled scrolled handles - Height 10"

Lotus Ware Valenciennes Jug - Fishnet pattern with applied twig handle - Height 3 1/2"

Lotus Ware Thebian Vase - Double gourd shaped form with applied step form handles - Height 8 1/4"

Lotus Ware Davenport Tea Set - Teapot, Sugar and
Creamer with hand painted flower pattern with
matching lids - Artist signed: A. Ferber - Height of
Teapot 5 1/4"

Lotus Ware Fan Pin Tray - Fan shaped dish with
woman laying on edge

Lotus Ware Columbia Bowl - Bulbous body with
ruffled rim and beaded ring near the top - Artist
signed: A.A. - Height 4 1/4"

Lotus Ware Umbrian Vase - Bulbous body with
short neck to flared top and applied scrolled
handles - Artist signed: M.I.W. 1897 to IDA M.
WALLACE - Height 8 1/4"

Lotus Ware Avignon Rose Jar - Bulbous body with
heavily decorated raised filigree ribbing throughout body and raised beaded rim - Lid has raised
beaded base with raised filigree form and finial top
- Height 6 1/4"

Lotus Ware Fern Jardiniere - Deep rounded bowl with ruffled mouth - Flower and leaf design with applied twig handles - Height 5 1/2"

Opposite Page Photo: Lotus Ware Roman Vase - Bulbous body with slender neck and flared top - Applied four looping handles and pale green flowers, leaves and stems - Height 10"

Lotus Ware Valenciennes Sugar and Creamer Set - Fishnet pattern with applied twig handle - Artist signed: A.G.M. - Height of Creamer 4 1/4"

Lotus Ware Shell Tray - Large shell with ruffled
edges and tri-footed base - Artist signed: M.A.B. -
Width 8 1/2"

Lotus Ware Roman Vase - Bulbous body with
slender neck and flared top - Applied four looping
handles and hand painted flower design - Height
10"

Lotus Ware Savonian Vase - Large vase with
bulbous body leading to elegantly designed lip
attached to applied fancy handles - Height 15 1/2"

Lotus Ware Columbia Bowl - Ovoid bowl with narrow mouth and ruffled beaded rim with bead line near the top - Applied filigree medallions on sides - Height 4 1/2"

Lotus Ware Quincy Chocolate Jug - Long tapering form body with spout and applied handle - Lip is matching with twig handle - Height 8 1/2"

Lotus Ware Shell Tray - Large shell with ruffled
edges and tri-footed base - Width 8 1/2"

Lotus Ware Lotus Tea - Tea cup with applied
handle - Artist signed: GRANDMA KERR -
Height 2 1/2"

Lotus Ware Valenciennes Jug - Fishnet pattern
with applied twig handle - Height 3 3/4"

Lotus Ware Laconian Vase - Ovoid form with ruffled lip on raised tear drop string design pedestal base - Four large raised filigree medallions mid-vase with four small raised filigree medallions between - Raised tear drop and jeweled strings throughout vase - Height 13"

Lotus Ware Ionian Vase - Large vase with bulbous body leading to elegantly designed lip attached to applied fancy handles and pedestal base - Height 18"

Lotus Ware Columbia Bowl - Bulbous body with fishnet pattern and ruffled beaded rim - Height 4"

Lotus Ware Tuscan Vase - Cylindrical style with filigree ribbing around bottom - Beaded rim and beaded star design around mid-vase with tri-footed base - Height 8"

Lotus Ware Columbia Bowl - Bublous body with
beaded ruffled rim and beaded ring near the top -
Fish scale pattern near the top with flowers and
branches - Height 4 1/2"

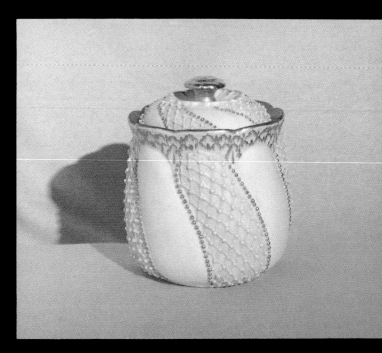

Lotus Ware Cracker Jar - Fishnet pattern with
matching lid - Height 6 3/4"

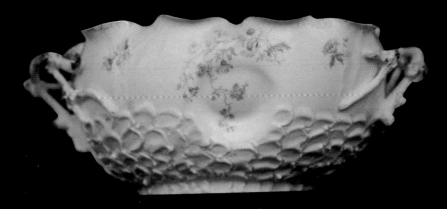

Lotus Ware Rustic Jardiniere - Deep round bowl with ruffled mouth and applied twig handles - Bottom half with fishnet pattern - Height 5 1/2"

Lotus Ware Columbia Bowl - Bulbous body with raised flower pattern and ruffled rim - Height 4 1/2"

Lotus Ware Venetian Vase - V-shaped form neck
with applied handles - Old man of the mountain
face on sides with petal design near lip and
columned base - Height 8"

Lotus Ware Coral Photo Holder - Coral shaped pattern with shell back - Height 4 3/4"

Lotus Ware Thebian Vase - Double gourd shaped form with applied step form handles - Height 8 1/4"

Lotus Ware Laconian Vase - Ovoid form with
ruffled lip - Four large raised filigree medallions
mid-vase with raised teardrop and jeweled strings
throughout vase - Height 10 1/4" - This piece was
exhibited at the Henry Ford Museum in October,
1960 in the "Americana, Midwest Collector's
Choice". The entry states, "Made as a presentation
piece for John N. Taylor's Wife of Knowles,
Taylor & Knowles Co., East Liverpool, Ohio,
Circa 1893.

Lotus Ware, Valenciennes Jug - Eichner pattern
with applied twig handle - Height 4"

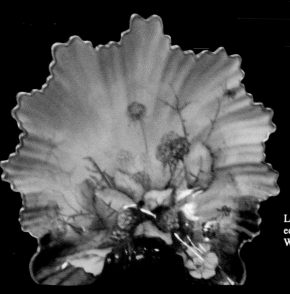

Lotus Ware Shell Tray - Large shell with ruffled edges and tri-footed base - Artist signed: W.W. - Width 8 1/2"

Lotus Ware Cracker Jar - Fishnet pattern with matching lid - Height 6 1/2"

Lotus Ware Ivica Jar - Bulbous body with circular
beaded base and beaded ring around the top - Lid
has raised beaded base with raised filigree form
and finial - Height 6 1/4"

Lotus Ware Tuscan Vase - Cylindrical vase with
flower and branch pattern on tri-footed base -
Height 8"

Lotus Ware Globe Jug - Flower pattern throughout
body with applied twig handle - Height 3 1/2"

Lotus Ware Etruscan Vase - Bulbous body with
slender neck to flared petal top with beaded base -
Applied scrolled handles with filigree medallions
on both sides - Beaded column from middle to top
- Amateur painted and non-glazed - Height 8"

Lotus Ware Globe Jug - Flowers and Victorian
Lady with Cherubs -Applied twig handle - Height
3 1/2"

Lotus Ware Tuscan Vase - Cylindrical style with fishnet pattern on tri-footed base - Height 8"

Lotus Ware Venetian Vase - V-shaped form neck with applied handles - Old man of the mountain face on sides with petal design near lip and columned base - Height 8"

Lotus Ware Columbia Bowl - Bulbous body with
beaded ruffled rim and beaded ring near the top -
Applied filigree medallions on sides - Height
4 1/2"

Opposite Page Photo: Lotus Ware Roman Vase -
Bulbous body with slender neck and flared top -
Applied four looping handles and hand painted
flower design - Height 10"

Lotus Ware Parmian Vase - Bulbous body with
long slender neck to flared ridged top - Swirled
scrolled handles with applied flower cluster, leaves
and stems - Height 10"

Lotus Ware Columbia Bowl - Bulbous body with beaded ruffled rim and beaded ring near the top - Height 4 1/2"

Lotus Ware Tuscan Vase - Cylindrical style with
filigree ribbing around bottom - Beaded rim and
beaded star design around mid-vase with tri-footed
base - Height 8"

Lotus Ware Globe Jug - Flower pattern throughout
body with applied twig handle - Height 3 1/2"

Lotus Ware Columbia Bowl - Bulbous body with
beaded ruffled rim and beaded ring near pinched
top - Applied filigree medallions on sides - Height
4 1/2"

Lotus Ware Roman Vase - Bulbous body with slender neck and flared top - Applied four looping handles and white flower clusters, leaves and stems - Height 10"

Lotus Ware Columbia Bowl - Bulbous body with ruffled rim and beaded ring near the top - Height 4"

Lotus Ware Venetian Vase - V-shaped form neck
with applied handles - Old man of the mountain
face on sides with petal design near lip and
columned base - Height 8"

Lotus Ware Cracker Jar - Fishnet pattern with
matching lid - Artist signed: R.T.C. TO E.A.T.
12-25-1903 - Height 6 3/4"

Lotus Ware Tuscan Vase - Cylindrical style with
filigree ribbing around bottom - Beaded rim and
beaded star design around mid-vase with tri-footed
base - Height 8"

Lotus Ware Orleans Rose Jar - Bulbous body with
circular base -Heavily decorated with raised
filigree ribbing throughout body and raised beaded
rim - Lid has raised beaded base with raised
filigree form and finial top - Height 7 1/2"

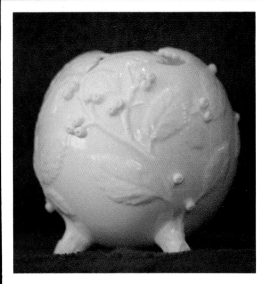

Lotus Ware Flower Bowl - Bulbous bowl with leaf and berry pattern with tri-footed base - Height 3 3/4"

Lotus Ware Columbia Bowl - Bulbous body with beaded ruffled rim - Artist signed: S.J.P. Height 4 1/4"

Lotus Ware Mecca A.D. Coffee Cup and Saucer -
Cup with applied handle and pattern on both cup
and saucer - Artist signed: E.W.B. "95" - Height of
Cup 2 1/2"

Lotus Ware Valenciennes Jug - Fishnet pattern
with twig handle - Height 4 1/2"

Lotus Ware Roman Vase - Bulbous body with
slender neck and flared top - Applied four looping
handles and pale green flowers, leaves and stems -
Height 10"

Lotus Ware Columbia Bowl - Fishnet pattern with
beaded ruffled rim - Artist signed: M.A.Clark -
Ellsworth, Maine - Height 4 1/4"

Lotus Ware Syrian Vase - Bulbous body with slender neck to patterned top - Applied scrolled handles - Artist signed: A. Walker 1907 - Height 7"

Lotus Ware Chestnut Sugar and Creamer - Creamer has small bulbous body with leaf pattern for spout and applied twig handle - Bowl follows same pattern with ruffled top - Height of Creamer 2 1/2"

Lotus Ware Columbia Bowl - Bulbous body with beaded ruffled pinched rim and beaded ring near the top with flower pattern - Applied filigree medallions on sides - Height 4 1/2"

Lotus Ware Valenciennes Jug - Flower and thorn branches throughout body with applied twig handle - Height 5"

Lotus Ware Columbia Bowl - Bulbous body with raised flower pattern and beaded ruffled rim - Height 4 1/2"

Lotus Ware Cracker Jar - Raised painted berries and flowers with branches and leaves - Lid is matching - Height 6 3/4"

Lotus Ware Egyptian Vase - Large vase with ovoid
body leading to narrow neck to a flared top -
Applied fancy handles with pedestal base - Filigree
medallions with raised tear drops and jeweled
strings - Height 15"

77

Lotus Ware Finger Bowl - Bulbous bowl with
ruffled rim - Artist signed: M.B. 96 - Height 2 1/2"

Lotus Ware Cracker Jar - Raised painted berries
and flowers with branches and leaves - Lid is
matching - Height 6 3/4"

Lotus Ware Savonian Vase - Large vase with
bulbous body leading to elegantly designed lip
attached to applied fancy handles - Height 15 1/2"

Lotus Ware Tuscan Vase - Cylindrical style with small fishnet pattern top and bottom - tri-footed base - Artist signed: WALKER 08 - Height 8"

Lotus Ware Globe Jug - Bulbous body with flower pattern and applied twig handle - Artist signed: M.V.F. XMAS 95 - Height 5"

Lotus Ware Columbia Bowl - Fishnet pattern with
ruffled beaded rim - Height 4 1/2"

Lotus Ware Globe Jug - Bulbous body with flower
pattern and applied twig handle - Height 4 1/4"

Lotus Ware Columbia Bowl - Bulbous body with beaded ruffled rim and beaded ring near the top with flower pattern - Applied filigree medallions on sides - Artist signed: DOT'94 - Height 4 1/2"

Lotus Ware Valenciennes Teapot, Sugar and Creamer - Fishnet pattern with applied twig handle and matching lids - Height of Teapot 5 1/4"

Lotus Ware Thebian Vase - Double gourd shaped form with applied step form handles - Applied white flowers clusters, leaves and stems - Height 8 1/4"

Lotus Ware Flower Bowl - Bulbous bowl with leaf and berry pattern with tri-footed base - Height 3 3/4"

Lotus Ware Chestnut Creamer - Small ovoid creamer with applied twig handle - Height 3 1/4"

Lotus Ware Rustic Jardiniere - Deep rounded bowl with ruffled mouth and applied twig handles - Applied nuggets with leaf pattern - Height 5"

Lotus Ware Etruscan Ewer - Bulbous body with
slender neck, applied scrolled handle and spout lip
- Filigree ribbing applied thoughout base with
beaded columns from middle to top - Height 9 1/2"

Lotus Ware Jewel Box - Bulbous body with raised
filigree medallions and beaded near the top - Lid
has raised filigree pattern with finial - Height
4 1/4"

Lotus Ware Tiberian Ewer - Bulbous body with
slender curved neck - Applied twig handle with
flower clusters, leaves and stems - Height 7"

Lotus Ware Oriental A.D. Coffee Cup and Saucer -
Leaf design on cup and saucer with applied twig
handle - Height of Cup 2 1/2"

Lotus Ware Tuscan Vase - Cylindrical style with
filigree ribbing around bottom - Beaded rim and
beaded star design around mid-vase with tri-footed
base - Height 8"

Lotus Ware Oriental A.D. Coffee Cup and Saucer -
Leaf design cup and saucer with applied twig
handle - Cup is dated on side Nov. 9th 1895 which
is the birthday of the owner - Base is marked
"XMAS" 1895 which was when the cup was given
to him - Height of Cup 2 1/2"

Lotus Ware Valenciennes Jug - Fishnet pattern
with applied twig handle - Height 3 3/4"

Lotus Ware Parmian Vase - Bulbous body with long slender neck to flared ridged top - Swirled scrolled handles - Height 10"

Lotus Ware Globe Jug - Flower pattern throughout body with applied twig handle - Height 2 1/2"

Lotus Ware Etruscan Vase - Bulbous body with
slender neck and applied scrolled handles - Height
8"

Lotus Ware Columbia Bowl - Bulbous body with beaded ruffled rim and beaded ring near pinched top - Applied filigree medallions on sides - Height 4 1/2"

Lotus Ware Venetian Vase - V-shaped form neck with applied handles - Old man of the mountain face on sides with petal design near lip and columned base - Height 8"

Lotus Ware Cracker Jar - Fishnet pattern with
matching lid - Height 6 1/2"

Lotus Ware Columbia Bowl - Bulbous body with
beaded ruffled rim and beaded ring near pinched
top - Applied filigree medallions on sides - Height
4 1/2"

Lotus Ware Globe Jug - Flower clusters through-out with applied twig handle - Artist signed: M.E.M. 1905 - Height 3 1/2"

Lotus Ware Umbriam Vase - Bulbous body with short neck to flared top and applied scrolled handles - Height 8 1/4"

Lotus Ware Vase - Bulbous body with ruffled rim
- Decorated with applied round chain forms and
small filigree raised forms - Height 7 1/2"

Lotus Ware Roman Vase - Bulbous body with
slender neck and flared top - Applied four looping
handles with cobalt and gilt design - Height
10 1/2"

Lotus Ware Umbrian Vase - Bulbous body with
short neck to flared top - Applied scrolled handles
with flower clusters, leaves and stems - Height
8 1/4"

Lotus Ware Columbia Bowl - Bulbous body with
beaded ruffled rim and beaded ring near pinched
top - Applied filigree medallions on sides - Height
4 1/4"

Lotus Ware Valenciennes Teapot, Sugar and
Creamer - Fishnet pattern with applied twig handle
and matching lids - Height of Teapot 5 1/4"

Lotus Ware Luxor Jar - Bulbous body with raised
filigree medallions on sides with dropped strings
and four petal type feet - Lid is matching with
finial - Height 7 1/4"

Lotus Ware Cremonian Vase - Small baluster form with applied scroll handles and fluted mouth - Height 6"

Lotus Ware Valenciennes Jug - Fishnet pattern with applied twig handle - Height 5"

Lotus Ware Bon Nappies - Large dish with leaf
pattern and ruffled rim - Height 2"

Lotus Ware Valenciennes Jug - Fishnet pattern
with applied twig handle - Artist signed: G.T.
DEC.14/94 - G.T. were the initials for Gedrae
Thomas - Height 3 1/2"

Lotus Ware Chestnut Creamer - Bulbous body with leaf pattern for spout and applied twig handle - Height 3 1/4"

Lotus Ware Chestnut Creamer - Bulbous body with leaf pattern for spout and applied twig handle - Height 3 1/4"

Lotus Ware Umbrian Vase - Bulbous body with
short neck to flared top - Applied scrolled handles
with flower clusters, leaves and stems - Height
8 1/4"

Lotus Ware Ivica Jar - Bulbous body with circular
beaded base and beaded ring around the top - Lid
has raised beaded base with raised filigree form
and finial - Height   6 1/4"

Lotus Ware Deccan Jar - Bulbous body with
filigree medallions on side and beaded ring near
base - Four petal feet with rosettes - Lid has
beaded base with raised filigree form and finial -
Height 7 1/4"

Lotus Ware Globe Jug - Flower pattern throughout
with applied twig handle - Artist signed: S.L.P.
XMAS 96 - Height 5"

Lotus Ware Globe Jug - Dutch type pattern with
applied twig handle - Artist signed: A.M.G. -
Height 3 3/4"

Lotus Ware Tuscan Vase - Cylindrical style with fishnet pattern on tri-footed base - Height 8"

Lotus Ware Columbia Bowl - Flower and branch pattern with beaded ruffled rim - Artist signed: AUG.1896 - Height 4 1/4"

Lotus Ware Tuscan Vase - Cylindrical style with
fishnet pattern on tri-footed base - Height 8"

Lotus Ware Globe Jug - Flower pattern throughout
body with applied twig handle - Height 3 1/2"

Lotus Ware Valenciennes Jug - Fishnet pattern with applied twig handle - Height 2 3/4"

Lotus Ware Valenciennes Teapot, Sugar and Creamer - Fishnet design with matching lids and applied twig handles - Height Teapot 5 1/4"

Lotus ware Etruscan Vase-Bulbous body with slender neck and applied scrolled handles-colors blue, green and pink on ends of fishnet-Height 8".

Lotus Ware Etruscan Ewer - Bulbous body with slender neck and applied scroll handle with spout lip - Height 9 3/4"

Lotus Ware Columbia Bowl - Bulbous body with
beaded ruffled rim and beaded ring near the top -
Applied filigree medallions on sides -Artist signed:
A.G.M. - Height 4 1/2"

Lotus Ware Fern Jardiniere - Deep rounded bowl
with ruffled mouth and applied twig handle - Hand
painted flower design with garlands of roses inside
- Artist signed: R.B. - Height 5 1/2"

Lotus Ware Globe Jug - Flower pattern throughout with applied twig handle - Artist signed: G.F. Mostelley - Height 3 1/2"

Lotus Ware Columbia Bowl - Bulbous body with flower pattern and beaded ruffled rim - Artist signed: N.Y.S. 1895 - Height 4 1/4"

Lotus Ware Globe Jug - Flower pattern throughout
with applied twig handle - Height 3 1/2"

Lotus Ware Oatmeal Nappie - Bowl with scalloped
rim - Height 1 3/4"

Lotus Ware Globe Jug - Flower pattern throughout
body with applied twig handle - Artist signed:
"RHODILICIALIL" - Height 5"

Lotus Ware Grecian Rose Jar - Bulbous body with heavily decorated raised filigree ribbing through-out body and raised beaded rim - Lid has raised beaded base with raised filigree form and finial top - Height 5 3/4"

Lotus Ware Thebian Vase - Double gourd shaped form with applied step form handles - Height 8 1/4"

Lotus Ware Etruscan Ewer-Bulbous body with slender neck, scrolled handle and spout lip-height 9 1/2".

114

Lotus Ware Grecian Rose Jar - Bulbous body with heavily decorated raised filigree ribbing throughout body and raised beaded rim - Lid has raised beaded base with raised filigree form and finial top - Height 6 1/4"

Lotus Ware Shell Tray - Medium shell with ruffled edges and tri-footed base - Width 5"

Lotus Ware Quincy Chocolate Jug- Long tapering form body with spout and applied handle - Lid is matching with twig handle - Height 8 1/2"

Lotus Ware GrecianVase - Bulbous body with slender pour spout with applied handle - Height 5 3/4"

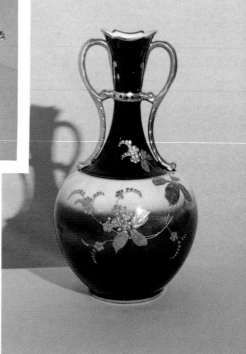

Lotus Ware Shell Tray - Large shell with ruffled edges and tri-footed base - Width 8 1/2"

Lotus Ware Etruscan Vase - Bulbous body with slender neck and applied scrolled handles - Height 8"

Lotus Ware Grecian Vase - Bulbous body with slender pour spout with applied handles - Height 5 3/4"

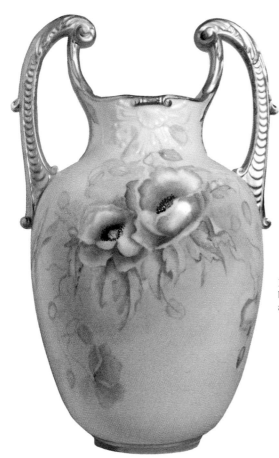

Lotus Ware Savonian Vase - Large vase with bulbous body leading to elegantly designed lip attached to applied fancy handles - Height 15 1/2"

Lotus Ware Tuscan Vase - Cylindrical style with fishnet pattern on tri-footed base - Height 8"

Lotus Ware Avignon Rose Jar - Bulbous body with heavily decorated raised filigree ribbing throughout body and raised beaded rim - Lid has raised beaded base with raised filigree form and finial top - Height 6 1/4"

Lotus Ware Quincy Chocolate Jug - Long tapering
form body with spout and applied handle - Lid is
matching with twig handle - Artist signed: H.B.
Windle 1893 - Height 8 1/2"

Lotus Ware Shell Salad - Large white shell dish
with coral feet - Width 8 1/2"

Lotus Ware Columbia Bowl - Bulbous body with beaded ruffled rim and beaded ring near the top with flower pattern - Artist signed: L.F.W. - Height 4 1/2"

Lotus Ware Clock Vase - Large oval frame on jeweled base with filigree medallions on sides - Jeweled flared top - Height 7"

Lotus Ware Etruscan Ewer - Bulbous body with slender neck, scroll handle and spout lip - Applied white flowers, leaves and stems - Height 9 1/2"

Lotus Ware Ionian Vase - Large vase with bulbous body leading to elegantly designed lip attached to applied fancy handles and pedestal base - Height 18"

Lotus Ware Columbia Bowl - Bulbous body with beaded ruffled rim and beaded ring near top with flower pattern - Height 4 1/2"

Lotus Ware Pedestal Dish - Leaf pattern bowl with pedestal base and four hollowed arms to hold dish with flared ends - Height 6"

Lotus Ware Columbia Bowl - Bulbous body with beaded ruffled rim and beaded ring near top with flower and gilt pattern - Artist signed: P.V. 95 - Height 4 1/2"

Lotus Ware Columbia Bowl - Pinched bowl with beaded ruffled rim and beaded ring near the top with molded flower pattern - Applied filigree medallions - Artist signed: Sutton - Height 4 1/2"

Lotus Ware Jug - Bulbous body with fancy pouring spout and applied scrolled handle on four scrolled feet - Height 5 1/2"

Chapter 3
China Whiskey Jugs
Circa 1891-1929

In the late 1880s, the firm of Knowles, Taylor & Knowles perfected their porcelain manufacturing techniques. From the early 1890s until 1929, when the firm was forced into bankruptcy at the onset of the Depression, Knowles, Taylor & Knowles manufactured china whiskey jugs. Today they are a sought after collector's item whose price could not compare with the pennies that the jugs cost when newly made.

On April 4, 1891, the East Liverpool *Daily Crisis* ran an ad that stated "The G.W. Meredith Co. is offering its Diamond Club Pure Rye Whiskey in china jugs that will come in three sizes." This is the first known mention of china whiskey jugs being sold.

George W. Meredith of East Liverpool, Ohio, who until 1880 had worked for Knowles, Taylor & Knowles, rose to fame and fortune with his distribution of Meredith Diamond Club Pure Rye Whiskey. As a promotional item to his best customers, he packaged the whiskey in the beautiful china jugs. These jugs became very popular, probably due to Mr. Meredith's efforts, as he distributed them from coast to coast. Many a customer kept the elegant containers long after the contents were gone.

During this period of time, other American liquor distributors were looking for ways to attract customers to their products as well. The soft white sheen and fancy lettering of the Knowles, Taylor & Knowles china whiskey jug was the perfect vessel.

Two trademarks to look for to authenticate the jugs are the serpents head near the top of the handle and the K.T.K./CHINA mark stamped on the base.

The jugs have a characteristic bulbous shape which leads to a slender neck usually with gilt trimming around the lip and on the handle. Their transfers, sharp and artistic, are found in colors of blue, red, brown and green. Many times a jug will appear in several different colors.

Most of the Knowles, Taylor & Knowles china whiskey jugs are quart size but the Meredith jugs are found in quart, pint, half-pint and miniature 1 1/2" sizes.

Many of the jugs were hand painted by the artists of Knowles, Taylor & Knowles and by other individuals who purchased them from the factory or other outlets. The hand painted jugs were probably used as "special occasion" pieces to give to friends, relatives and employees, filled with special drinks such as ciders, wines, or home made blends of whiskey.

Although the whiskey jugs do not demand the high prices of the fine china made by Knowles, Taylor & Knowles, they do remind us of the skill required to make a utilitarian item a lasting thing of beauty.

The following are jugs known to the author. There are possibly other variations that exist.

Meredith - Diamond Club - Quart jug in green

IT TASTES GOOD

MEREDITH'S DIAMOND CLUB PURE RYE WHISKEY tastes good, looks good and is good. It is put up in the most attractive jugs and bottles. Its outside appearance is fine, and its inside contents are finer still.

MEREDITH'S
DIAMOND CLUB
Pure Rye Whiskey

Maintains its standard always. The quality does not go up and down with the thermometer. What you buy to-day is the same as you bought a year ago. What you buy next year will be the same as you buy to-day. This whiskey took the highest award over all bottled whiskies at the World's Fair. It possesses age, mellowness, mildness. There is pleasure in every drop. Its purity makes it the safest whiskey on earth for medicinal use. These are facts that you cannot afford to ignore.

65c Per Pint $1.25 Per Quart
Sold Everywhere
Send for Our Booklet

G. W. MEREDITH & CO.
Largest Whiskey Bottlers in America
EAST LIVERPOOL, - - OHIO.

Meredith - Diamond Club - Pint in green

Meredith - Diamond Club - Half-pint jug in green

Meredith - Diamond Club - One and one half inch height - in green

Meredith - Diamond Club 1880 - Quart jug in green - 1880 is the age of the rye not the jug

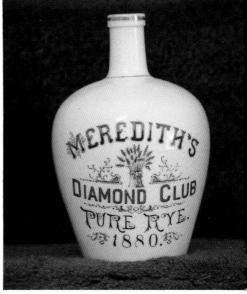

Meredith - Diamond Club 1880 - Quart jug in red

Opposite Page Photo: Meredith - Diamond Club - Quart jug in green - Absence of East Liverpool, Ohio address near base possibly indicates Meredith's move to Pittsburgh, Pennsylvania around 1908 as East Liverpool was voted dry on July 23, 1907

MEREDITH'S
DIAMOND CLUB

TRADE
MARK

PURE RYE
WHISKEY.

EXPRESSLY FOR
MEDICINAL USE.

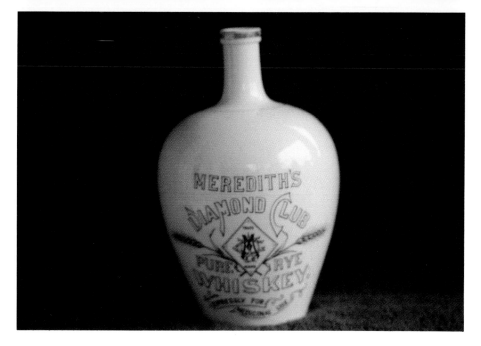

Meredith - Diamond Club - Quart jug in green -
Note absence of East Liverpool, Ohio near base
and different style of letters

Quart jug with initials A.W. which stood for
Ambrose Webber who was on the Board of
Directors for the G.W. Meredith Co. - Jeresy
Apple was probably his favorite drink

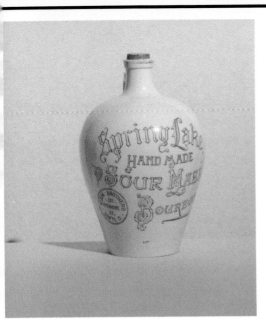

Spring Lake - Sour Mash Bourbon - Klein Bros.
121 Sycamore St. Cinti, Ohio - Quart jug in red -
Distributor of whiskey in 1887 - Became Klein
Bros. & Hyman from 1887 to 1897 - Became Klein
Bros. again in 1898

Spring Lake - Sour Mash Bourbon - Klein Bros. &
Hyman 17 Sycamore St. Cinti, Ohio - Quart jug in
red

Spring Lake - Sour Mash Bourbon - Klein Bros.
121 Sycamore St. Cinti, Ohio - Quart jug in green

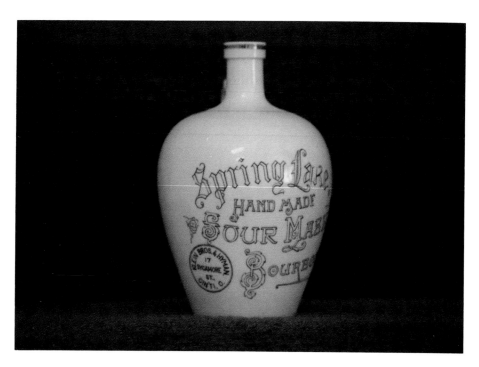

Spring Lake - Sour Mash Bourbon - Klein Bros. &
Hyman 17 Sycamore St. Cinti, Ohio - Quart jug in
green

Unusual jug with Klein Bros. & Hyman 17
Sycamore St. Cinti, Ohio in circle with a large "B"
for bourbon, and completed with hand painted red
roses - Quart jug in red

Spring Lake - Sour Mash Bourbon - Klein Bros. &
Hyman Cincinnati, Proprietors - Quart jug in blue

Old Maryland - Pure Rye Whiskey - G. Riesmeyer,
St.Louis, Mo. - Distributors of whiskey 1901-1918
- Quart jug in brown

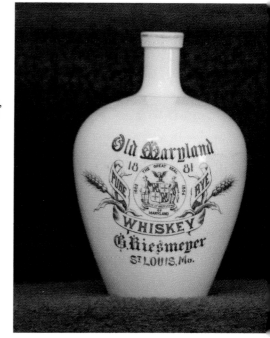

Old Maryland - Pure Rye Whiskey - G. Reismeyer,
St. Louis, Mo. - Quart jug in blue

Pennsylvania Club - Pure Rye Whiskey - Quart jug in red - Pennsylvania Club name was registered to M.L. Wolf, Philadelphia, Pennsylvania, in 1895

Pennsylvania Club - Pure Rye - Quart jug in green

Urban Club - Sour Mash Bourbon - A. Urban &
Son, Quincy, Ill. - Quart jug in red - Bourbon was
distilled by Union Distilling Co. Cincinnati, Ohio -
1883-1917

John Limegrover Jr. - Pure Rye Whiskey - 44 Ohio
St. - Allegheny -"Sherwood" in circle - Quart jug
in green - Sherwood was registered 1879 to Hyatt
and Clark Distillers, Baltimore, Maryland and in
1905 to Sherwood Distillers, Baltimore, Maryland

J. A. Dougherty's Sons,

—— DISTILLERS OF ——

PURE RYE WHISKY.

Offices:

Nos. 1136 and 1138
NORTH FRONT STREET.

Distillery and Heated Bonded Warehouses: 1128 to 1146 NORTH FRONT ST., West Side; 1121 to 1133 NORTH FRONT ST., East Side; 1125 to 1143 HOPE ST.
Malt House: 1135 and 1137 NORTH FRONT ST.
Cooper Shops: 1124 and 1126 NORTH FRONT ST.; 1121 and 1123 HOPE ST.

PHILADELPHIA, PA.

New York Representative: **L. L. HYNEMAN, 118 WALNUT ST., PHILADELPHIA.**

John Limegrover Jr. - Pure Rye Whiskey - 44 Ohio
St. - Allegheny -"Dougherty's" in circle - Quart jug
in red - Dougherty's Distiller was registered in
1894 by J.A. Dougherty & Son, Philadelphia,
Pennsylvania

ANDREW M. MOORE   JOSEPH F. SINNOTT

ESTABLISHED 1837

GIBSONTON MILLS
ON THE MONONGAHELA RIVER

MOORE & SINNOTT
P-OPPIETORS AND
SUCCESSORS TO   John Gibson's Son & Co.
DISTILLERS OF FINE WHISKIES

GIBSONTON MILLS ON THE MONONGAHELA RIVER
ERECTED 1856.

OUR DISTILLERY AT GIBSONTON
On the Monongahela River, with its Extensive Kilns and Malt
Houses, gives us Unequaled Facilities for Distilling

PURE MONONGAHELA RYE, WHEAT AND MALT

WHISKIES

Of Superior Quality, from Kiln-Dried Grain and Barley Malt
WE HAVE ON HAND

**THE LARGEST AND BEST STOCK OF CHOICE OLD WHISKIES IN
THE UNITED STATES, all of which are highly improved by age**

Storage Capacity in Heated Bonded Warehouses, · · · 50,000 Bbls.

PRINCIPAL OFFICE

232 and 234 South Front Street, PHILADELPHIA

AGENCIES
| NEW YORK | BOSTON | NEW ORLEANS | SAN FRANCISCO |
| 62 Broad St. | 160 State St. | 102 Poydras St. | 314 Sacramento St. |

CHARLESTON, S. C.   SAVANNAH   AUGUSTA, GA.

John Limegrover Jr. - Pure Rye Whiskey - 44 Ohio
St. - Allegheny - "Gibson's" in circle - Quart jug in
green - Distilled by Moore & Sinnott, Philadelphia,
Pennsylvania from 1899

138

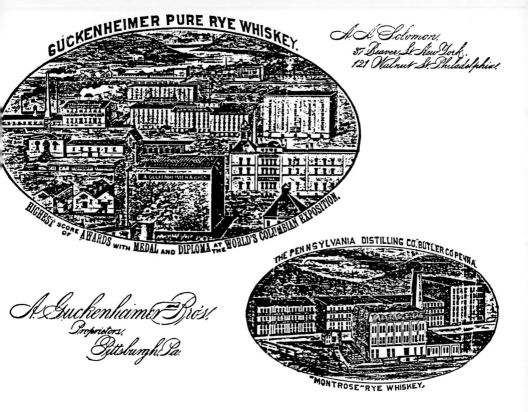

Getty & Co. - Old Premium Pure Rye Whiskies Pittsburgh, Pa. - Quart jug in green - Old Premium was the whiskey in the jug - The four names in the circle were four other brands Getty & Co. sold - Golden Wedding was first registered in 1882 and again in 1908 by the Joseph S. Finch Distillers, Pittsburgh, Pennsylvania, A. Guckenheimer & Bros. Distillery, Pittsburgh, Penn. 1891-1918

139

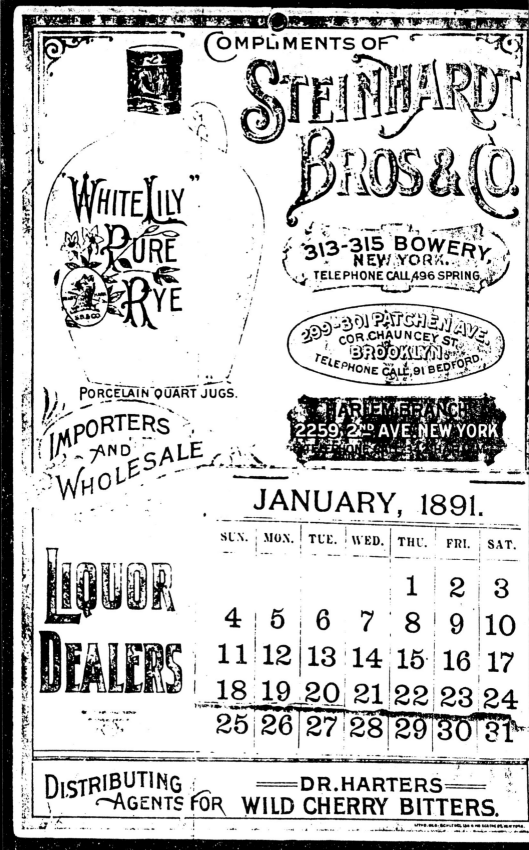

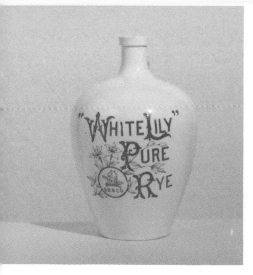

White Lily - Pure Rye with S.B & Co. in yellow circle showing a mythical beast with a spear in its neck - Quart jug in blue - S.B.& Co. - Steinhardt Bros., New York Distributors of White Lily Rye from the late 1800s until the early 1900s

White Lily - Pure Rye - Quart jug in red

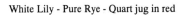

White Lily - Pure Rye - Quart jug in green

Mike & Jim's Private Stock 1881 - Pure Rye
Whiskey - Quart jug in green - Private Stock was
registered in 1897 to Edward Walters Distillers,
Baltimore, Maryland

Old Times - Sour Mash Bourbon - H. Mayer,
Waco, Texas, Proprietor - Old Times Distiller,
Louisville, Kentucky - 1870-1914 - Brand was not
registered until 1905

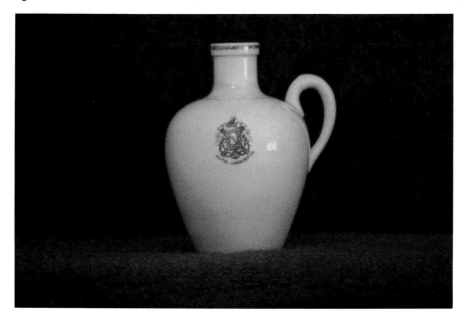

Hotel Lafayette - One half pint jug in green - crest
has been identified as the Coat of Arms of the
Marquis De Lafayette and the hotel site as Hotel
Lafayette, Marietta, Ohio

Monk holding glass of wine with his dinner - Quart
jug with reddish brown body

Back view of monk jug showing a smoking pipe

Quart jug hand painted - Pictures two red nosed
males drinking whiskey from a keg, with the
shorter male standing on the keg

Back view of jug shows sheafs of grain with words
"Original Package"

147

F.C. Karcher's Private Little Jug - Quart jug in gilt
script

Pint jug hand decorated with painted Victorian
Lady and silver overlay with pewter stopper

Quart jug with hand painted flower design

Quart jug with dark blue base and white flower
design

Quart jug with pink flower design

Quart jug with matte finish and strawberry design

Quart jug with twin handles and cream matte finish
with blue wisteria flower design

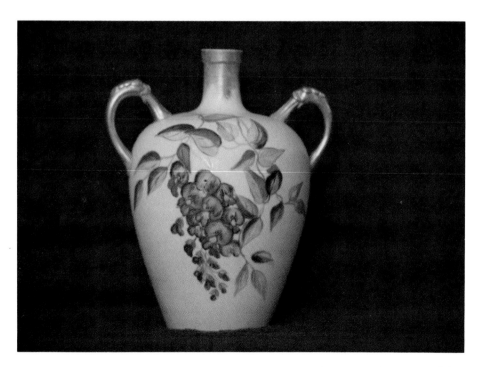

Quart jug with twin handles and cream matte finish
with violet wisteria flower design

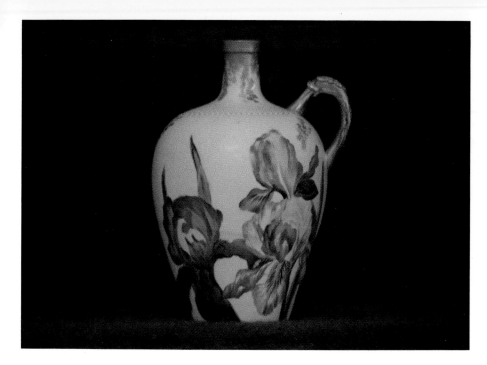

Quart jug with violet flower design

Quart jug with yellow flower design

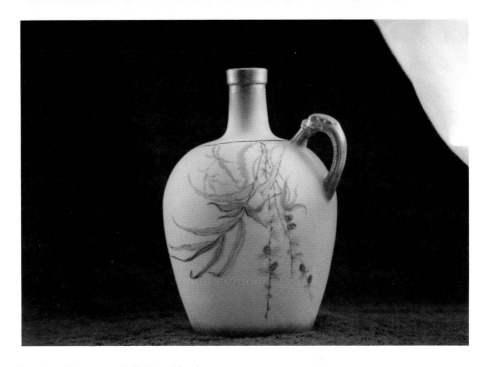

Quart jug with cream matte finish and fern leaves
with pine cone branches

Quart jug with cream matte finish and flower
design

Quart jug with cream matte finish and pine cone
branches

Quart jug with cream matte finish and purple
flower design

Bibliography

"A Little History of Pottery Making", Crockery and Glass Journal, Dec. 20, 1917, pp. 55-56.

Boger, Louise, *The Dictionary of World Pottery and Porcelain,* New York: Charles Scribner and Sons, 1971.

Edmonson, Barbara, "Old Advertising Spirits Glasses," Maverick Publication, 1988.

Gates, William C., *The City of Hills and Kilns; Life and Work in East Liverpool, Ohio,* Published by East Liverpool Historical Society, 1984.

New Encyclopaedia Britannica - 15th Edition, Vol. 2, 1992.

Snyder Whiskey Research Center, Amarillo, Texas; Robert Snyder, 1992.

Sullivan, Jack, K.T. & K. Whiskey Jugs. Antique Bottle and Glass Collector, 1990.

$\mathcal{I}$ndex

℞rice Guide

Values vary immensley according to the condition of the piece, the location of the market, and the overall quality of the design and manufacture. Condition is always of paramount importance in assigning a value. Prices vary by geographic location and those at specialty antique shows will vary from those at general shows.

To use this reference well it is necessary to know that the left hand number is the **page** number. The letters following it indicate the **position** of the photograph on the page: T=top, L=left, TL=top left, TC=top center, TR=top right, C=center, CL=center left, CR=center right, R=right, B=bottom, BL=bottom left, BC=bottom center, and BR=bottom right. The last numbers are the estimated **value** ranges in U.S. dollars.